Many Friends Cooking

An International Cookbook for Boys and Girls

Cooked and Written by

Terry Touff Cooper & Marilyn Ratner

Illustrated by

Tony Chen

PHILOMEL BOOKS

in cooperation with the U.S. Committee for UNICEF
New York

Text copyright © 1980 by Terry Touff Cooper and Marilyn Ratner. Illustrations copyright © 1980 by Tony Chen. All rights reserved. Manufactured in the United States of America.
ISBN 0-399-20755-4   U.S. Committee for UNICEF ISBN 0–935738–00–2

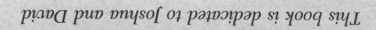

This book is dedicated to Joshua and David

A Note to Young Cooks

Celebrate a Swedish holiday with Surprise Rice Pudding. Lunch Italian-style on Hero Sandwiches. Sip a taste of China with Won Ton Soup. The recipes in this book link you with the cooks and customs of many lands. If you've cooked with our first cookbook, *Many Hands Cooking*, you will already be familiar with some international foods. In this book you'll discover delicious new tastes and foods and even new ways of eating—with chopsticks, for instance.

We have tried to keep the recipes as authentic as possible; however, some have been adapted for young cooks. Each one has a code—one, two, or three spoons—to give you an idea of its difficulty. (See page v.) Most of the ingredients in the recipes are available in supermarkets, but a few call for a trip to a health-food store or specialty food market.

Before starting to cook, read the sections on safety and measuring and the helpful hints. And while you're cooking, don't hesitate to look back at the cooking terms and equipment if you come across something that you're not sure of.

On many pages you'll notice people wearing their national costumes. These costumes are a beautiful part of a country's culture and history. Of course, in most countries today, these clothes are worn only for holidays and special events.

We hope you will enjoy using this book. Have fun!

Each numbered country on the map matches the page number of a country (and a recipe) listed below on the Contents page—for example, 1 is Lebanon, 5 is the United States, 15 is Argentina, and so forth.

Contents

YOU BE THE JUDGE. Each recipe has a code.

❘ (one spoon) recipes are the easiest to make.

❘❘ (two spoons) recipes are easy to make.

❘❘❘ (three spoons) recipes are not hard, but do take a little extra time and work.

If you've never cooked before, start with a one-spoon recipe. You'll soon find that you can easily make even those rated by three spoons. If you can follow directions, you can learn to cook anything.

SAFETY FIRST

Always use a pot holder or oven mitts in handling any hot pots or pans.

Ask someone older to help you to light the oven or stove—until you have learned how to do it safely yourself.

Keep the handles of any pots or pans cooking on the stove turned inward. That way you won't knock over hot food by accident.

Always pick up a knife by its handle, not by its blade.

When you've finished cooking, make sure all oven and stove dials are turned OFF.

GETTING STARTED

Whether or not you've cooked before, these tips will help you tackle a recipe.

1. Read the recipe from start to finish and see if you have everything you need.
2. Make a shopping list.
3. Buy the needed ingredients.
4. Wash your hands before handling food.
5. Get out all the ingredients and put them near your work space.
6. Gather the cooking equipment you need.
7. Read the recipe again. Look up any kitchen terms you aren't sure of on pages ix–x.
8. For best results, always follow the recipe exactly at first. After that, you can try variations.
9. If you have a kitchen timer, use it. Then you'll be sure to bake or cook your food the right length of time.
10. *Have fun!*

Helpful Hints

A Word About Ingredients

Most of the ingredients used in these recipes are available at the supermarket. In a few cases a trip to the specialty gourmet food shop or health-food store might be necessary and fun. If you can't find an ingredient, study the recipe and see if it can be left out. If not, maybe a substitute ingredient would do.

How to Cook Rice

1 cup of raw long-grained rice makes 2 cups of cooked rice.

INGREDIENTS

1 cup long-grained rice   1¾ cups cold water

EQUIPMENT

measuring cup   fork
medium saucepan and lid

HOW TO MAKE:

1. Place the rice in the saucepan and cover with the cold water.
2. Bring the water and rice to a boil. Cover the pan and turn heat very low.
3. Cook the rice for 15–20 minutes, until the water is absorbed. Check to see that the rice isn't too dry after 15 minutes. Turn off the heat, but leave the lid on for 5 minutes.
4. Fluff the rice with the fork.

How to Deep Fry

Deep frying is cooking food in a deep layer of hot oil. Ask an adult or older friend to help you if you have never done this before. It's best to use a deep-fat fryer, a high-sided pan with a removable wire basket. You can also use a high-sided frying pan, but be sure it is large enough and deep enough so that the oil will not splatter. If you have an electric deep-fat fryer, follow the manufacturer's directions.

Fry the food in vegetable oil and use enough oil to cover it completely. The oil should be at least 3 inches below the top of the pan, so that it won't bubble over.

To fry, pour the oil into the fryer. Heat the oil. To test whether the oil is hot enough, gently drop in a bit of the batter or food to be fried or a small bread cube. Always use a spoon or tongs and oven mitts to protect your hands. If the food pops to the top of the oil, the temperature is right. If it browns immediately, the oil is too hot.

After the fried food is cooked, remove it to paper towels so that any extra fat can be absorbed. Bring the oil back to the right temperature before continuing.

How to Separate Eggs

Have two bowls, one for the yolks, one for the whites. Crack open the egg by hitting it against the hard edge of a bowl. Gently pull the shell apart, and let the white drop into the bowl, keeping the yolk back in one half of the shell. Carefully pour the yolk back and forth from one half of the eggshell to the other to free all the white from the yolk. Drop the yolk alone into the other bowl.

How to Peel Tomatoes

Tomato skin loosens and peels off easily if you lower the tomatoes very carefully, one at a time, into boiling water to cover. You may want to ask an adult or older friend to help you with this. Boil the tomatoes for 3 seconds. Remove them from the water with tongs or a slotted spoon, let them cool, and peel them.

How to Whip Cream

It's best if both the bowl and the beater are chilled.

INGREDIENTS

½ pint heavy cream	½ t. vanilla
1 T. sugar	

EQUIPMENT

medium mixing bowl	egg beater or electric beater
mixing spoon	

HOW TO MAKE:

1. Pour the cream into the bowl and beat until it thickens and forms soft peaks.
2. Gently fold in the sugar and vanilla.

Kitchen Terms to Know

BAKE. To cook in an oven.

BASTE. To moisten with liquid while cooking.

BATTER. An uncooked mixture of flour, liquid, and other ingredients, as for a cake or pancakes.

BEAT. To make foods smooth or light by stirring with an over-and-over motion. Usually done with a fork or mixing spoon.

BLEND. To mix thoroughly two or more ingredients, usually with a spoon.

BOIL. To cook on top of the stove at a point where large bubbles come to the surface and break. To heat liquid to this point is to bring to a boil.

BROIL. To cook under or over direct heat—under a stove's broiler or over an open fire or grill.

BROWN. To cook until brown in color.

CHILL. To cool in the refrigerator.

CHOP. To cut up into small pieces with an up-and-down motion, using a knife or chopper. To chop into finer pieces is to mince.

COMBINE. To mix ingredients together.

COOL. To let hot food stand until it feels cool.

CRUSH. To pound into small pieces.

CUBE. To cut into small blocks, from ½ in. by ½ in. to 1 in. by 1 in. in size.

DASH. Less than ⅛ t. of a dry ingredient.

DECORATE. To dress up a dish by using nuts, parsley, olives, etc.

DEEP FRY. To cook in a deep layer of fat or oil.

DICE. To cut into small cubes less than ½ in. in size.

DRAIN. To pour off liquid.

FLOUR. (1) To roll food in flour. (2) To sprinkle a greased baking pan with a little flour; then shake until the flour lightly covers the pan. Pour off any extra flour.

FLUFF. To lift gently with a fork so that pieces separate.

FOLD. To mix gently by lifting from bottom to top, then folding over.

FRY. To cook in a layer of fat or oil.

GRATE. To rub food against a grater, so that it breaks into small pieces. Watch your knuckles!

GREASE. To smear a baking pan with a small amount of butter or shortening. Use clean fingers or a crumpled piece of waxed paper.

MARINATE. To soak in liquid.

MASH. To squash with the back of a fork or spoon until soft and smooth.

MEASURE. To put the amount called for in a recipe into a measuring cup or spoon.

MELT. To heat a solid food, such as butter or chocolate, until it turns liquid.

MINCE. To cut into pieces finer than chopped. Use the same motion as for chopping but do it for a longer time.

MIX. To stir ingredients together, usually with a spoon.

MIXTURE. A combination of ingredients.

PEEL. To strip off the outer layer or skin. Use hands for bananas and oranges; a paring knife for cucumbers and avocados.

PINCH. The amount you can hold between your thumb and first finger.

PREHEAT. To heat the oven to the temperature called for in the recipe before putting the food in to roast or bake.

SAUTÉ. To cook on top of the stove in a small amount of fat.

SET. To let stand until firm.

SIFT. To put dry ingredients, such as flour, through a sifter or strainer.

SIMMER. To cook gently on top of the stove just below the boiling point. Small bubbles appear around the edge of the liquid, but the surface moves only slightly.

SLICE. To cut into thin pieces with a knife.

SOAK. To cover with liquid and let stand.

SOFTEN. To leave butter or margarine at room temperature for 15 to 30 minutes, so that it becomes soft and easy to use.

SPRINKLE. To scatter on top of another food.

STIR. To move around and around with a spoon.

THAW. To leave frozen food at room temperature so that it unfreezes.

TOAST. To brown and dry surfaces of food such as bread or sesame seeds.

TOSS. To mix together by lifting and turning.

WHIP. To beat rapidly such foods as eggs or cream, so that they become mixed with air, thicken, and expand.

Measuring Made Simple

To measure dry ingredients—flour, sugar, etc. Fill the right-sized measuring cup or spoon until it overflows. Then pull a straight-edged knife across the top to level off.

To measure liquids in a cup—milk, water, etc. Set measuring cup on a flat surface. Pour in liquid until full or fill to desired mark.

To measure liquids in a spoon—vanilla, etc. Pour liquid into right-sized measuring spoon until full.

To measure butter. One stick or ¼ lb. of butter is equal to ½ cup or 8 tablespoons. Half a stick equals ¼ cup or 4 tablespoons. To measure 2 tablespoons, cut off one quarter of a ¼-pound stick.

Abbreviations Used in the Recipes

in.	=	inch	qt. = quart
lb.	=	pound	T. = tablespoon
oz.	=	ounce	t. = teaspoon
pkg.	=	package	F. = Fahrenheit
pt.	=	pint	

Table of Measures

dash = less than ⅛ teaspoon, 1 shake of salt, pepper, or other seasoning

pinch = amount you can pick up between tip of first finger and thumb

3 teaspoons = 1 tablespoon

4 tablespoons = ¼ cup

8 tablespoons = ½ cup

1 cup = ½ pint or 8 ounces

2 cups = 1 pint or 16 ounces

16 ounces = 1 pound

4 cups = 2 pints or 1 quart

4 quarts = 1 gallon

Handy Cooking Tools

FOR PREPARING FOOD

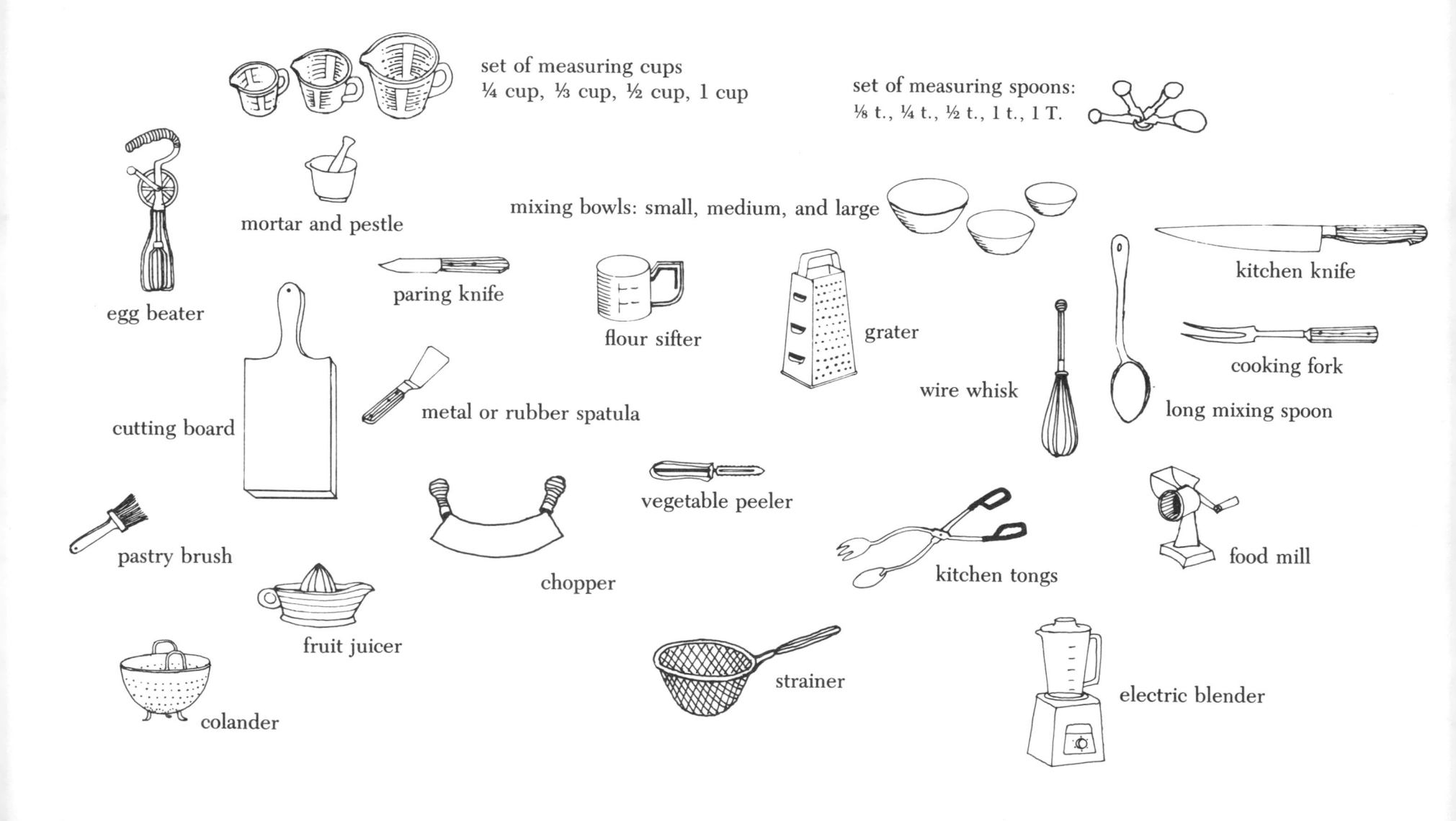

set of measuring cups
¼ cup, ⅓ cup, ½ cup, 1 cup

set of measuring spoons:
⅛ t., ¼ t., ½ t., 1 t., 1 T.

mortar and pestle

mixing bowls: small, medium, and large

egg beater

paring knife

flour sifter

grater

kitchen knife

cutting board

metal or rubber spatula

wire whisk

long mixing spoon

cooking fork

pastry brush

chopper

vegetable peeler

kitchen tongs

food mill

fruit juicer

strainer

electric blender

colander

FOR COOKING

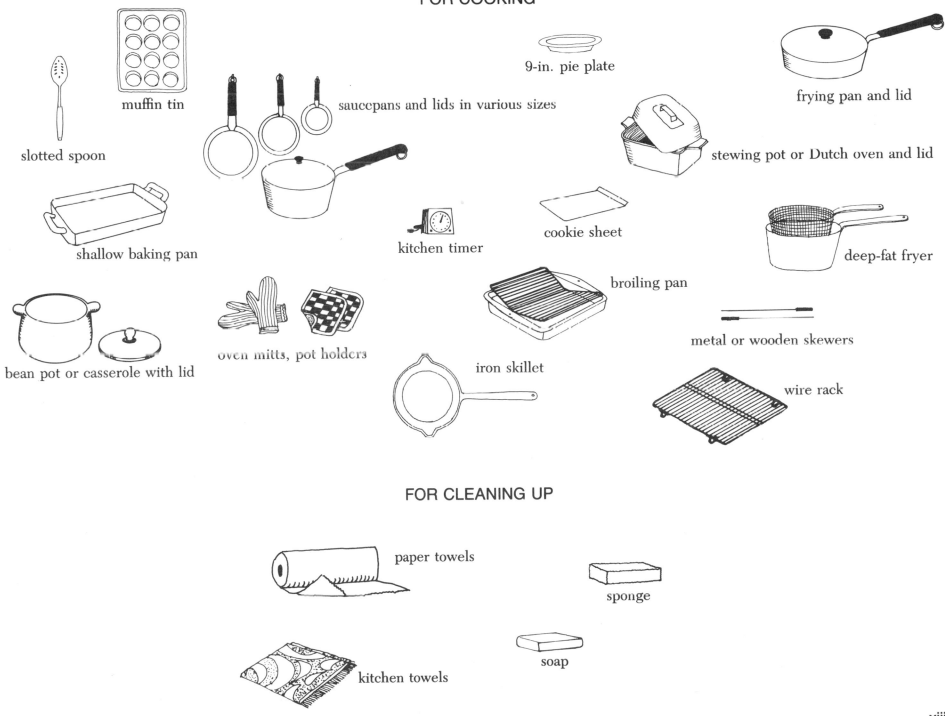

muffin tin

slotted spoon

saucepans and lids in various sizes

9-in. pie plate

frying pan and lid

stewing pot or Dutch oven and lid

shallow baking pan

kitchen timer

cookie sheet

deep-fat fryer

bean pot or casserole with lid

oven mitts, pot holders

broiling pan

metal or wooden skewers

iron skillet

wire rack

FOR CLEANING UP

paper towels

sponge

kitchen towels

soap

Four Fancy Napkin Foldings

Napkins have been popular at different times in history. The Romans were early napkin users. Then napkins disappeared for a time. In the Middle Ages they reappeared in the form of a large-sized communal napkin, which was attached to the edge of the table for all the diners to use. In time, as forks grew popular and fingers stayed cleaner, napkins became decorative as well as useful.

During the seventeenth century, Europeans placed much importance on setting a proper table, and settlers brought the practice to America. Napkin folding became an art. Elaborate designs were devised. But the folded napkins were only to be admired, not used.

Try the napkin foldings below. You can admire *and* use them. Fold them for a party or a family meal. It's best to use napkins that are about 16 inches square.

THE FAN

1. Fold the napkin in half to form a rectangle.
2. Pleat the napkin with accordion pleats.
3. Place the bottom of the napkin in a glass and spread out the pleats.

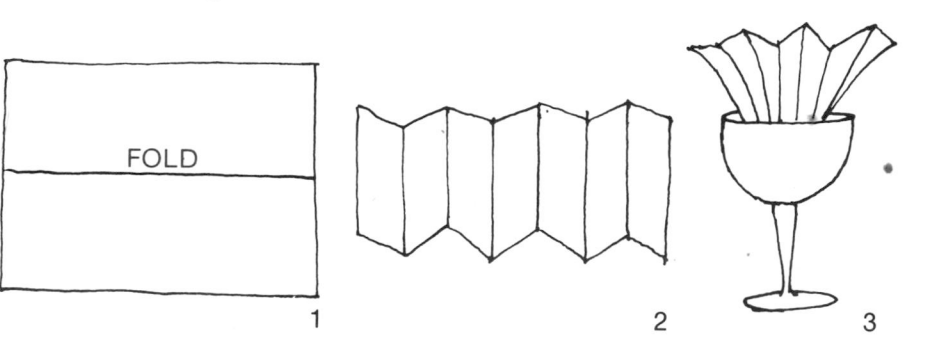

THE BOAT

1. Fold the napkin in half to form a triangle.
2. Fold sides A and C toward the center to form a middle triangle B. Ends A and C will hang down.
3. Fold up points A and C so that they are even with the base of the triangle.
4. Fold over the base of the triangle to form a boat.

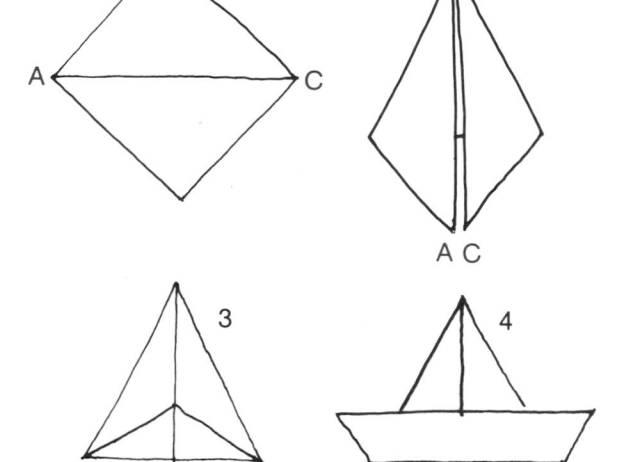

THE FLOWER

1. Fold the napkin in quarters.
2. Fold the napkin in half to form a triangle (*see The Boat*).
3. Fold sides A and C toward the center to form a middle triangle B. Ends A and C will hang down (*see The Boat*).
4. Fold back points A and C so that they are even with the base of the triangle at the back of the napkin. You cannot see the folded points.
5. Fold the napkin in half lengthwise. Fold it away from you so that you are looking at the crease.
6. Hold the base tightly in one hand. With the other hand peel half the layers of the napkin toward you and the other half away from you.
7. Set the napkin on the table resting on its base.

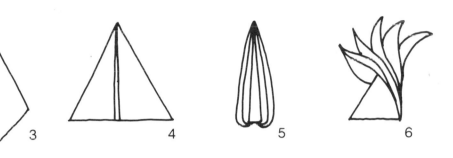

SILVERWARE POCKET

1. Fold the napkin in quarters.
2. Turn the napkin so that the loose corners are at the top and the original center of the napkin is at the bottom.
3. Fold the top layer down to meet the bottom of the triangle. This makes a pocket.
4. Fold under sides A and B. Slip the silverware into the pocket.

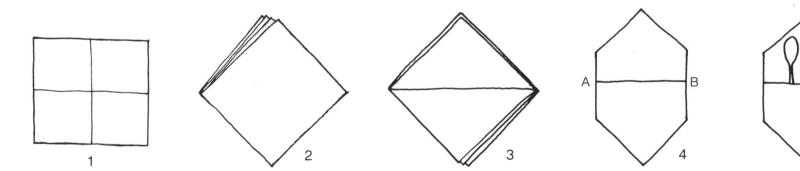

Around the World Eating Customs

Have you ever noticed how your family eats? If not, take note. Do family members sit on chairs around a table or do they sit on the floor? Do they eat with knives, forks and spoons or with their fingers? Do they talk to each other while they eat? People in different countries often have different eating habits. Here are some:

INDIA: In India the rule is that you never use the left hand for eating. Only the fingers of your right hand may touch the food. And your fingers may dip into the food only up to the first knuckle.

KOREA: Koreans love to eat and spend much time preparing and enjoying their meals. They consider eating so important that they like to put all their attention to it. So until the meal is finished it is the custom in Korea to talk as little as possible.

JAPAN: In Japanese rooms there are no chairs. So family and guests kneel or sit cross-legged on cushions at a low table in their stockinged feet. Before the meal diners receive a tightly rolled hand towel dampened with very hot water to wipe their hands and face. This towel is called the *oshi bori*.

GHANA: Be sure never to talk, hum or sing while dining in Ghana. It's bad luck if you do. And it's added bad luck to let the third finger of your right hand touch your nose while eating.

INDONESIA: At an Indonesian meal you'll need to follow these rules for eating. Before each bite you must dip the fingers of your right hand into a finger bowl of water. Then roll food such as mashed vegetables or rice into small bite-sized balls. Place the food in your mouth. But don't let the food touch the palm of your hand and don't let your fingers enter your mouth.

Chopsticks Made Simple

Chopsticks have a history that is longer than the Great Wall of China. They were first used in ancient Japan and China.

The Chinese say you can tell a lot about people by the way they use their chopsticks:

- If a Chinese baby girl first grasps chopsticks at the far end, her future husband lives far away.
- If you drop your chopsticks, you will have bad luck.
- If your chopsticks are not the same length, you will miss a boat or a train.

Not all chopsticks are alike. The Chinese kind are longer than the Japanese chopsticks and have blunt ends. Japanese chopsticks have pointed ends and are more tapered.

Have you ever tried eating with chopsticks? Did you struggle to hold them and pick up food? Read the steps below and struggle no more:

1. Hold the upper chopstick between the thumb and first finger as if holding a pencil.
2. Position the lower chopstick in the crook of the thumb resting on the fourth finger.
3. Move the upper chopstick to pick up food. The lower one remains still.

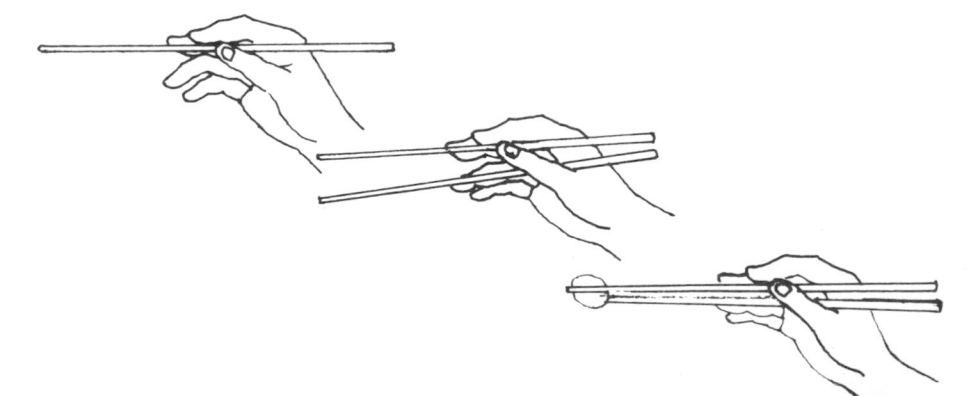

Herbs and Spices

Salt, pepper, dill, nutmeg, cinnamon, and parsley are a few of the many herbs and spices used in this book. Each has its own fascinating story about where it came from and how it was used in the past. Add some historical flavor to your cooking by reading the herb and spice stories below.

DILL (an herb): The name *dill* comes from the Norwegian "dilla" meaning "to lull." For hundreds of years dill was used to soothe or heal. It was said that dill helped to cure upset stomachs and hiccups. Long ago soldiers placed burned dill seeds on wounds to help them heal. Gardeners around the twelfth century raised dill to use in love potions and to cast spells. At that time, a person often carried a bag of dill over his or her heart to keep evil away.

PEPPER (a spice): Pepper was first used some 4,000 years ago in India. It is probably the oldest known spice, and was for many years the most valuable. Pepper was carried westward by traders who often used it as a substitute for money. A single peppercorn was valued like a jewel. Taxes and rents were often paid in pepper. (Can you imagine counting out peppercorns to pay a storekeeper for an ice-cream cone?)

GARLIC (an herb): Garlic appears in Greek mythology as a means to ward off evil spirits. Physicians of ancient Greece prescribed it for treating wounds and cleaning the blood. Romans fed garlic to their athletes to give them strength and courage.

Some even say that in high mountain regions where the air is thin, cloves of garlic placed in the nose will help bring enough oxygen into the body.

PARSLEY (an herb): This herb is said to be a symbol of joy, festivity, and honor. Greeks crowned heroes with it. Romans not only ate it, but decorated their dining halls with it. They believed it sweetened the breath. Some people still do.

Parsley stems have been used to make green dye. The herb has also been known to fasten false teeth, put a sparkle in dim eyes, and relieve a cramp in the side.

Is it an herb? Herbs are mostly aromatic, leafy plants that are used as a medicine, flavoring, or seasoning.

Is it a spice? Spices are generally dried for use and usually come from Oriental trees.

INTERNATIONAL SANDWICH SPREAD

The sandwich goes a long way back. Here are some historic sandwich highlights:

- Arabs stuffed envelopelike loaves of bread called *pitas* with barbecued meat. Pita-stuffers were the first to come up with a practical leakproof sandwich.
- Before the Aztecs, ancient peoples of Mexico rolled vegetables, meat, and fruit into corn tortillas.
- In the Middle Ages, thick blocks of bread were piled high with meat and other foods and served on wooden trenchers. Might these have been the first open-faced sandwiches?
- The Fourth Earl of Sandwich, who lived in the eighteenth century, was the first person in the Western world to put meat or cheese between two slices of bread. In this way he could keep his hands grease-and-fork-free while he played cards. The word *sandwich* comes from the name of this card-playing earl.

Bring the sandwich up to date by making the international favorites on these pages. Invite some friends over to share them with you. Then move the sandwich into the future by inventing creations of your own.

From

Lebanon
STUFFED PITA POCKETS
Serves 6 to 8

INGREDIENTS

1	medium onion
2	medium tomatoes
2	T. butter
1	pound ground beef or lamb

1	t. salt
½	t. pepper
2	T. chopped dill or parsley
1	pita bread for each sandwich
	lettuce leaves

EQUIPMENT

paring knife
measuring spoons
large frying pan

mixing spoon
slotted spoon
plate

HOW TO MAKE:

1. Chop the onion fine. Cut the tomatoes into small pieces.
2. Melt the butter in a frying pan. Sauté the onion for 5 minutes.
3. Add the meat, salt, pepper, dill or parsley, and chopped tomatoes. Mix well.
4. Cook over medium heat, breaking the meat up with a spoon and stirring all the time until the meat browns.
5. Use slotted spoon to remove mixture from the pan to the plate.
6. Slice pita bread in half and stuff each pocket with a lettuce leaf and heaping spoonfuls of the meat-and-tomato mixture.

NOTE: Pita bread is sold in many large supermarkets and food specialty stores. Sometimes it is called Middle Eastern flat bread or Sahara bread.

1

From

Italy

HERO SANDWICHES

Serves 2

INGREDIENTS

1 Italian sandwich loaf or ½ loaf of Italian bread
4 lettuce leaves
2 T. salad oil
1 t. vinegar
8 slices of salami
6 slices of tomato
6 slices of cheese, such as Provolone or Mozzarella

EQUIPMENT

knife
paper towels
measuring spoons
small bowl

HOW TO MAKE:

1. Cut the bread in half the long way.
2. Wash lettuce leaves and pat dry with towels.
3. Lay leaves on bread. Sprinkle lettuce with oil and vinegar.
4. Lay other ingredients on top in any order you wish.
5. Cut into two sandwiches and serve.

For a hot hero, wrap the sandwich in foil and warm in a 250° F. oven for 10 minutes.

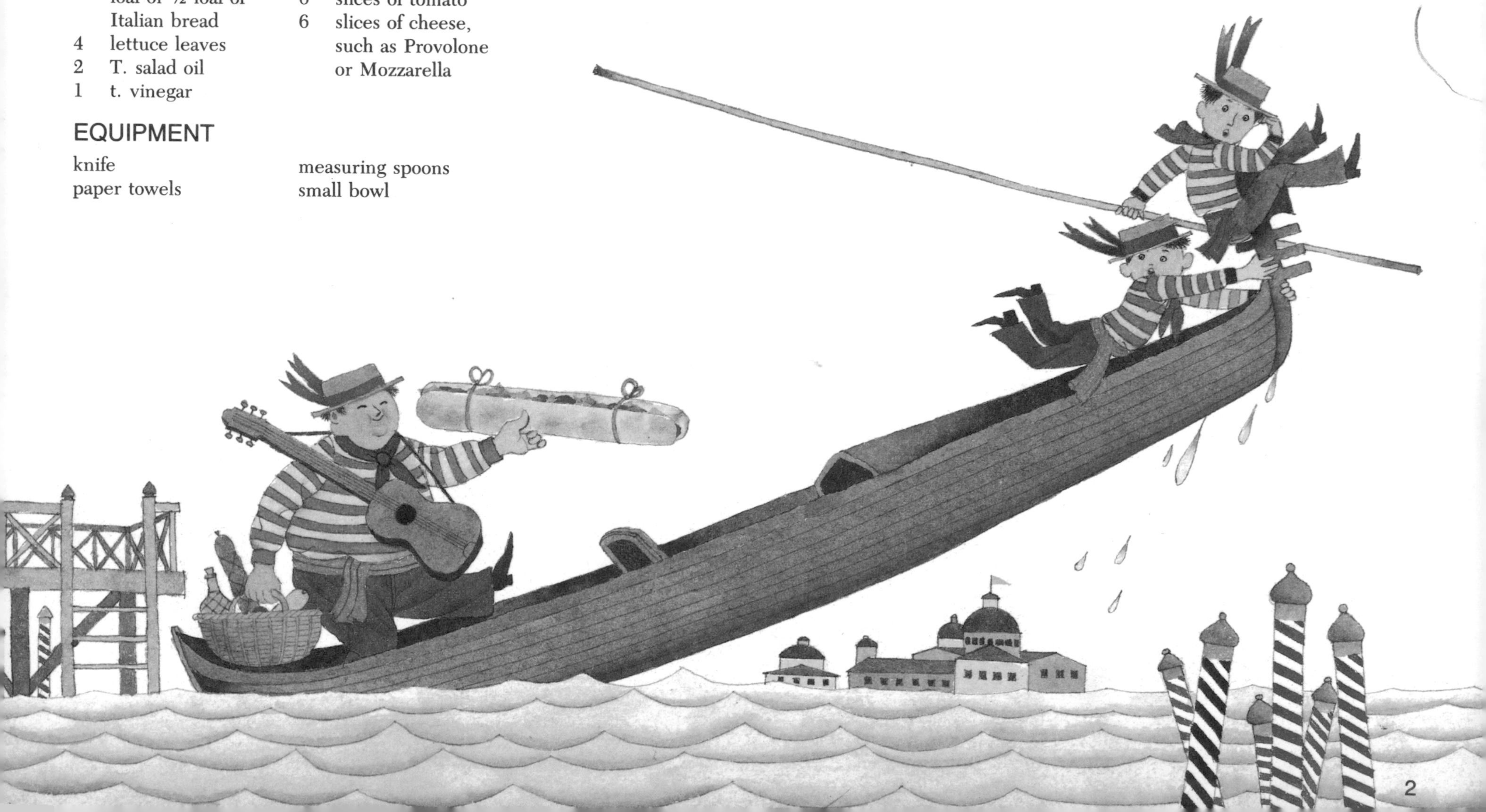

From
Mexico

BURRITOS—Little Burros

Serves 4

INGREDIENTS

1	onion
2	T. butter
¼	lb. ground beef
2	oz. Cheddar cheese
8	oz. can refried beans
3	T. vegetable oil
4	to 8 tortillas

EQUIPMENT

paring knife
measuring spoons
frying pan
fork or spatula

slotted spoon
mixing bowl
grater
measuring cups

HOW TO MAKE:

1. Peel and mince the onion. Melt the butter in the frying pan over low heat. Add the onion and sauté until soft.

2. Add the ground beef and cook, stirring with a fork or spatula, until the beef is browned.

3. Spoon the mixture into a bowl, draining the grease off as you do it.

4. Grate the cheese and open the refried beans. Add both to the mixture and stir.

5. Wash the frying pan, put it back on the stove, and add 3 tablespoons of oil. Turn on the burner to low heat.

6. Spoon about 3 tablespoons of the mixture into the center of each tortilla, fold each tortilla in half, and then fold the corners into the center (see illustration). Fry the stuffed tortillas on both sides until crisp.

3

the United States

RIO GRANDE CHILI
Serves 4 🍴🍴

Hey, partner. Shake that dust off your boots, mosey on over to the campfire and have a bowl of fire—chili, that is. This cattle-country dish most likely began with a chili pepper from the chuck wagon. Cooks in the early nineteenth century added whatever other ingredients they had on hand to the campfire brew, and you can, too. There are hundreds of ways to make chili.

No matter which way you choose, do beware. Go easy on the chili powder, or be prepared to put out the fire in your mouth.

INGREDIENTS

1 onion	1 16-oz. can kidney
2 T. butter	beans
1 lb. ground beef	1 t. chili powder
⅛ t. garlic powder	1 t. salt
2 cups water	⅛ t. basil
1 16-oz. can	1 bay leaf
tomatoes with juice	

EQUIPMENT

paring knife	mixing spoon
frying pan	large saucepan
measuring spoons	measuring cups

HOW TO MAKE:

1. Peel and chop onion. Melt the butter in the frying pan over low heat. Add onion and sauté until soft and golden.
2. Add the meat and stir until browned.
3. Put meat mixture in a large saucepan and add remaining ingredients. Simmer until sauce has become thick, about one hour. Stir often.

There are as many ways to cook Boston Baked Beans as there are New England cooks. Some flavor the pot with a peeled onion; others add a chunk of pork. Some cooks use brown sugar; others, molasses or maple syrup. Family recipes for baked beans have been handed down since Colonial times when this hearty dish was a Sabbath specialty. Why? No work was to be done on the Sabbath, so on Saturday morning a great pot of beans was set to cook. The first helpings were for Saturday supper. Then the leftovers were put back in the oven to keep warm for after-church Sunday lunch.

INGREDIENTS

1 lb. (2 cups) white kidney beans or navy beans	4 oz. lean salt pork or bacon
12 cups water (for soaking and cooking)	¼ cup molasses
	1 T. sugar
2 t. salt	¼ t. dry mustard

EQUIPMENT

pot to soak and cook the beans	paring knife
measuring cups	bean pot or casserole with lid
measuring spoons	mixing spoon

HOW TO MAKE:

1. Place the beans in the pot. Add 6 cups of water and soak the beans overnight.
2. Drain off the water and add 6 cups of fresh water. Add the salt and bring the beans to a boil. Lower the heat to simmer and cook the beans for 1 to 2 hours until they are tender. Taste a bean for tenderness.
3. Dice the salt pork or bacon.
4. Preheat the oven to 275° F.
5. Transfer the beans to the bean pot or casserole. Add the salt pork or bacon. Stir in the molasses, sugar, and mustard.
6. Next add enough boiling water to cover the mixture. Cover the bean pot and bake the beans for 6 to 8 hours. During the last ½ hour, remove the cover so that a crusty top forms.

NOTE: This dish may be baked days ahead, refrigerated, and reheated.

If you are using canned beans instead of cooking the beans from scratch, start with step 3.

the United States

"What's for dessert?" is a common question in the United States, a dessert-minded country. In the North, it might be apple pie. In the Southern states, especially Louisiana and Georgia, pecan pie is a favorite. Nearly every Southern cook has a recipe for pecan pie. Here is a classic version. Serve it with freshly made whipped cream. (See page viii for directions.)

INGREDIENTS

3	eggs	1	t. vanilla
2	T. sugar	¼	t. salt
2	T. flour	1½	cups pecans
2	cups dark corn syrup	1	unbaked 9-inch pie shell

EQUIPMENT

mixing bowl	measuring cups
egg beater	measuring spoons
mixing spoon	9-inch pie plate

HOW TO MAKE:

1. Preheat the oven to 425° F.
2. In the mixing bowl, beat the eggs with the egg beater until light and fluffy.
3. Add the sugar, flour, corn syrup, vanilla, and salt, and beat well.
4. Break pecans into small pieces and stir into the mixture.
5. Place unbaked pie shell in a pie plate and pour in the filling.
6. Bake at 425° for 10 minutes. Reduce heat to 325°. Bake 40 minutes more. Cool and serve.

From

the United States

SNICKERDOODLES

Makes about 3 dozen cookies

Bake a batch of crinkle cookies. German settlers in the United States, many of whom found homes in the Midwest, contributed these easy-to-bake treats to American cookie jars. Earliest cookbooks call them Schnecken Noodles, but late nineteenth-century cookbooks, especially those from Kentucky and Missouri, list them as Snickerdoodles. Whatever you call them, you'll want to fill your cookie jar with these cinnamon-sprinkled drop cookies.

INGREDIENTS

3	cups all-purpose flour	1	t. vanilla
½	t. salt	2	eggs
¾	t. baking soda	¼	cup milk
1	cup soft butter or margarine (2 sticks)	1	T. butter for cookie sheets
		For Topping	
1½	cups sugar	3	T. sugar
		3	T. cinnamon

EQUIPMENT

measuring cups	mixing spoon
measuring spoons	fork or egg beater
flour sifter	2 small bowls
medium mixing bowl	teaspoon
large mixing bowl	2 cookie sheets

HOW TO MAKE:

1. Preheat oven to 375° F.
2. Sift flour, salt, and baking soda into the medium mixing bowl and set aside.
3. Put the butter or margarine into the large mixing bowl and cream it well. Then add the sugar, a little at a time, beating until smooth. Stir in the vanilla.
4. Beat the eggs in one of the small bowls. Add the beaten eggs to the butter and sugar mixture.
5. Add the milk and the sifted dry ingredients to the egg, butter, and sugar mixture. Stir to combine.
6. Combine the sugar and cinnamon for the topping in the second small bowl.
7. Grease the cookie sheets with the butter.
8. Drop large teaspoonfuls of dough onto the greased cookie sheets about 1 inch apart. Use your finger or another spoon to get the dough off the teaspoon. Sprinkle the tops of the cookies with cinnamon and sugar.
9. Bake about 10 minutes until cookies brown around the edges.
10. Remove from oven and loosen cookies from sheets while still warm.
11. When cookies are cool, store in an airtight container.

VARIATIONS: Add one or more of these to cookie dough: 1 cup chopped nuts, ½ cup raisins, ½ cup currants.

Say "Lea Lea Kakou." It means "to happiness" in Hawaiian and is a traditional Luau toast. For your next Hawaiian feast or Luau, raise glasses filled with this refreshing punch and toast good fortune to all.

INGREDIENTS

1   orange
¼ cup sugar
½ t. whole cloves
1   cup water

3   cups pineapple or grapefruit juice
1½ cups orange juice

EQUIPMENT

paring knife
pitcher that can hold boiling water

measuring cups
measuring spoons

HOW TO MAKE:

1. Slice the orange into five or six slices. Put slices in the pitcher.
2. Sprinkle sugar over the orange slices.
3. Add cloves to the pitcher.
4. Boil the water. Pour the boiling water over the orange slices, sugar, and cloves. Let stand for five minutes.
5. Add the pineapple or grapefruit juice and the orange juice to the pitcher.
6. Chill for an hour before serving.

From
Cuba
ORANGE CHICKEN
Serves 4 to 6

A rainbow of citrus fruits ripen in the blazing sun of this tropical island. You can almost taste Cuba's sunshine in this tangy chicken bake. Add rice to the dish, invite friends to the table, and you'll all enjoy a delicious Latin American meal.

INGREDIENTS

1 chicken (3 to 3½ lbs.) cut into serving pieces
2 t. salt
1 t. pepper
½ t. garlic salt
2 cups orange juice
1 lime

EQUIPMENT

small mixing bowls
paring knife
measuring spoons
measuring cups
baking pan

HOW TO MAKE:

1. Measure salt, pepper, and garlic salt into the small bowl.
2. Sprinkle both sides of the chicken pieces with this mixture.
3. Measure the orange juice.
4. Cut the lime in half and squeeze the juice into the orange juice.
5. Place the chicken pieces in the baking pan and pour the orange-lime juice over the chicken. Marinate the chicken in the juice for 1 hour, then turn the pieces and marinate 1 hour longer.
6. Remove chicken from the pan. Pour the juice off into the bowl.
7. Preheat the oven to 350° F.
8. Return chicken to the baking pan and add ½ cup of the juice.
9. Bake for 30 minutes, then baste with 1 cup additional juice. Bake 30 minutes more or until chicken is tender.

11

From
Jamaica
COCONUT SHERBET
Serves 6 to 8

In Jamaica's sunny climate, coconut palms dot the land. They're nature's most useful trees. Why? Because every part of the coconut palm which thrives on this island has some value. Its sturdy nutshells are fashioned into spoons, cups, toys, and buttons. Oil from its dried-fruit kernels is used for products ranging from margarine to soap. And best of all, fresh coconut meat is used to flavor such sweets as this smooth sherbet.

You can buy coconut cream in cans in gourmet food markets and health-food stores. In Jamaica, grated coconut meat is covered with water and pressed through a sieve to make coconut cream.

INGREDIENTS

½ cup orange or pineapple juice	1½ cups skim milk
1 envelope un-flavored gelatin	¾ cup coconut cream

EQUIPMENT

saucepan	electric mixer or
measuring cups	egg beater
mixing spoon	plastic wrap
metal bowl	

HOW TO MAKE:

1. Mix the fruit juice and gelatin in a saucepan and stir over low heat until the gelatin dissolves.
2. Add the milk and coconut cream and stir to combine.
3. Pour the mixture into a metal bowl and place in the freezer for 1½ hours, or until partly frozen and still mushy.
4. With an electric mixer or egg beater, beat the mixture until it is smooth. Cover the bowl with plastic wrap and return to the freezer. Continue freezing several hours until hard.

Trinidad

BANANA MUFFINS

Makes 12 muffins

In the early sixteenth century, a missionary bound for the New World put some dry banana rootstocks into his baggage. Over the high seas to Santo Domingo came those first bananas. There they were planted and then carried by missionaries and traders to other Caribbean islands. Trinidad was one.

The people of this sun-bleached island like bananas in cakes, fritters, and stews. But that's just for starters. Bananas are added to any and every food and cooked in any and every way. Try them baked in muffins.

INGREDIENTS

¼ cup soft butter or margarine
½ cup sugar
2 eggs
2 overripe bananas
1 cup flour
½ t. baking soda
½ t. vanilla
1 T. butter or margarine for greasing muffin tin

EQUIPMENT

mixing bowl
measuring cups
egg beater
mixing spoon
flour sifter
measuring spoons
muffin tin

HOW TO MAKE:

1. Preheat oven to 350° F.
2. Put soft butter, sugar, and eggs in the mixing bowl and beat.
3. Break bananas into small pieces and add. Beat well.
4. Sift flour and baking soda and add to the batter. Beat in the vanilla. The batter should be smooth.
5. Grease each muffin cup with butter or margarine.
6. Use the mixing spoon or a measuring cup to fill each cup ⅔ full with batter.
7. Bake for 20 minutes, or until golden brown.

Argentina is famous for beef. Here's a meal-in-one-dish that combines beef, vegetables, and fruit. It's a tasty stew that can be cooked over a stove or campfire. In Argentina, dinner guests would have this dish served to them in a baked pumpkin. The pumpkin is brought to the table, and the stew ladled onto heated plates.

INGREDIENTS

2	lbs. beef chuck or stew meat
1	large onion
2	green peppers
3	tomatoes
6	potatoes
3	ears corn or 1 cup canned corn
3	T. vegetable oil
4	cups beef broth
1	bay leaf
1	T. oregano
	salt and pepper to taste
4	peaches or apples

EQUIPMENT

sharp knife	plate
paring knife	measuring cups
Dutch oven or large saucepan with lid	measuring spoons
mixing spoon	

HOW TO MAKE:

1. Cut the beef into 1-inch cubes.
2. Prepare the vegetables: peel and chop the onion, chop the green pepper and tomatoes; peel and cut the potatoes into ½-inch cubes; shuck the corn and cut into 1-inch rounds.
3. Heat the oil in the Dutch oven or saucepan over medium heat. Add the cubes of meat and brown on all sides by turning over with the mixing spoon. When the meat is brown, remove it to a plate.
4. Add the onions and green pepper to the pan and cook until soft, about 5 minutes.
5. Add the beef broth and bring to a boil. Return the beef to the pan and add the tomatoes, potatoes, and seasonings.
6. Cover the pan, reduce heat to simmer, and cook for 1½ hours.
7. While the stew is cooking, peel and slice the peaches or apples.
8. Add the corn and fruit to the stew and cook for 5 minutes longer.
9. Serve on heated plates or from a heated serving dish.

From
Chile HUEVOS RANCHEROS
Ranch-Style Eggs
Serves 2

For workers on dairy farms or big ranches, a hearty midday meal is a must. When Chileans break for lunch, ranch-style eggs, steak, and hot cocoa make an unmatchable meal. You could make this brightly colored dish for a spicy Sunday breakfast or brunch with a friend.

INGREDIENTS

1	onion	1	t. sugar
2	medium tomatoes or 3 to 4 canned Italian plum tomatoes	¼	t. salt
			dash of black pepper
1	serrano chili (available in cans)	2	tortillas
		1	T. butter
3	T. vegetable oil	2	eggs

EQUIPMENT

paring knife   mixing bowl
measuring spoons   paper towels
frying pan   spatula

HOW TO MAKE:

1. Peel and mince the onion. Chop the tomatoes. Rinse the chili in cold water and mince.
2. Heat 2 tablespoons of the oil in the frying pan; add vegetables, sugar, salt and pepper. Cook over low heat for 10 to 15 minutes until the vegetables are soft. Most of the tomato juices will evaporate, leaving a thick sauce.
3. Pour the sauce into the mixing bowl. Wash and dry the frying pan.
4. To cook the tortillas, heat 1 tablespoon of oil in the frying pan over low heat. Fry one tortilla at a time for one minute on each side. Turn with the spatula. Drain the tortillas on the paper towels.
5. Let the frying pan cool. Wipe out with a paper towel.
6. Melt 1 tablespoon butter in the frying pan. Crack eggs into the pan, and fry until the whites are set but the yolks are still soft.
7. Use spatula to place one egg on each tortilla. Spoon the sauce around each egg.

From
Bolivia
LITTLE COCOA PEAKS
Makes 16 mini-cakes

Have you ever tasted a mountain? Here's your chance. The gently rising chocolate peaks in this recipe reflect the high mountains and plateaus that stretch through the heartland of Bolivia and the rich cocoa beans that grow there. If you want your mountains to be snow-covered, top them with ice cream or whipped cream. (See directions page viii.)

INGREDIENTS

½ cup soft butter or margarine
1 cup sugar
3 eggs
¾ cup cocoa
1¾ cups flour
1 T. baking powder
pinch of salt
⅔ cup milk
1 t. vanilla
1 T. butter or margarine for greasing muffin tin

EQUIPMENT

measuring cups
large mixing bowl
mixing spoon
small bowl
egg beater
measuring spoons
flour sifter
muffin tin
table knife
wire rack

HOW TO MAKE:

1. Put the butter, or margarine, and sugar into the large mixing bowl and beat well.
2. In the small bowl beat the eggs with the egg beater until light. Then, with the mixing spoon, beat the eggs into the butter and sugar mixture.
3. Sift the cocoa, 1½ cups flour, baking powder, and salt.
4. Measure out the milk.
5. Add half the dry ingredients to the large mixing bowl. Beat well. Now add half the milk and beat. Add the rest of the dry ingredients. Beat well. Add the rest of the milk and beat.
6. Stir in the vanilla.
7. Preheat the oven to 375° F.
8. Butter the muffin tin. Sprinkle a little of the remaining ¼ cup of flour into each cup and shake the tin until flour coats each cup.
9. Pour the batter into each muffin cup, filling each ⅔ full.
10. Bake for 20 minutes.
11. Remove from oven and cut around the edge of each mini-cake with a knife in order to loosen it. Gently turn the muffin tin over. The cakes will drop out.
12. Cool on a wire rack or serve warm topped with whipped cream or ice cream.

A VARIATION: You might add walnuts or pecans to the batter—½ cup chopped.

It's foolproof! With this simple entrée from France, you can't go wrong for brunch, lunch, or dinner. It's a pie without a crust, filled with vegetables, mixed with eggs, and then baked till puffed and brown. Add any combination of vegetables, such as potatoes, zucchini, cauliflower, or carrots. A traditional quiche is cooked in a pastry shell. You can cook yours this way, too. If you do, be sure to use a 9-inch shell.

INGREDIENTS

1	medium onion	⅛	cup vegetable oil
2	tomatoes	4	eggs
1	small eggplant or		dash garlic salt
	2 medium zucchini	½	cup milk
12	mushrooms	1	T. flour
¼	cup Parmesan		salt and pepper
	cheese		to taste
12	oz. Swiss cheese		

EQUIPMENT

paring knife	mixing spoon
measuring cups	mixing bowl
grater	fork
large iron skillet	measuring spoons

HOW TO MAKE:

1. Peel and chop the onion, tomatoes, eggplant, or zucchini. Wash and slice the mushrooms. Grate the cheeses.
2. Heat the oil in the skillet over low heat. [NOTE: If you don't have an iron skillet, you can sauté the vegetables in a frying pan and add the other ingredients. Then pour the mixture into a greased 8-inch-square baking pan or a 9-inch pie plate to bake in the oven.]
3. Add the vegetables and stir for 15 minutes until the vegetables are soft.
4. Preheat the oven to 400° F.
5. Beat the eggs with the fork and add to the mixture. Add the garlic salt, milk, flour, cheeses, salt and pepper. Combine well.
6. Put the skillet in the oven for 25 minutes. Cut the quiche into wedges to serve.

From

Spain

GAZPACHO—Cold Fresh
Vegetable Soup
Serves 6

Cool off in hot summer weather. The Spanish know how, with a cold salad you can sip—gazpacho. Chop and mix fresh tomato, cucumber, and green pepper. Season and chill. You're set for a drinkable feast. In Spain, different towns make different versions of this soup. After you make this one, invent your own gazpacho by adding any of your favorite vegetables.

INGREDIENTS

2	cucumbers	2	cups cold water
5	medium tomatoes	2	cups tomato juice
1	onion	¼	cup olive oil
1	green pepper	1	T. salt
2	cloves garlic		

EQUIPMENT

paring knife   measuring cups
large mixing bowl   blender or food mill
mixing spoon   fork

HOW TO MAKE:

1. Peel cucumbers and cut into pieces. Peel tomatoes (for directions, see page viii) and onion and chop coarsely. Cut green pepper into small pieces. Peel garlic and chop fine.
2. In a large mixing bowl combine chopped cucumbers, tomatoes, onion, green pepper, and garlic. Mix well.
3. Stir in water and tomato juice.
4. Pour the mixture into a blender 2 cups at a time and blend at high speed for 1 minute. If using a food mill, pour mixture in small amounts and purée.
5. Pour all of the puréed mixture into a mixing bowl. Beat in the olive oil with the fork. Add salt.
6. Cover the bowl and refrigerate. Chill and serve very cold.

Sweden
SURPRISE RICE PUDDING
Serves 6 to 8 🥄🥄

Christmas Eve in Sweden. Friends and families have gathered together. Candles flicker. Faces glow. Everyone's ready for a holiday game of chance. This is the way it is played: Creamy rice pudding is spooned into bowls and passed around. Everyone watches. Waits. When each person has been served, the eating begins . . . slowly . . . carefully.

Legend says that the person who finds an almond in his or her pudding will have good luck and good fortune all the year long. You might serve this rice pudding at a party. The finder of the almond might also be given a prize.

INGREDIENTS

3	T. butter	4	T. sugar
1	cup rice	¼	t. salt
¾	cup water	1	t. vanilla
1	qt. milk	1	whole almond
1	cinnamon stick, or		
	1 t. cinnamon		

EQUIPMENT

measuring spoons   measuring cups
saucepan   mixing spoon

HOW TO MAKE:

1. Melt the butter in the saucepan. Add the rice and water. Bring to a boil and cook, stirring with the mixing spoon, for about 5 minutes.
2. Add the milk, cinnamon, sugar, salt, and vanilla.
3. Simmer for about 20 minutes, stirring every few minutes. Be careful not to let the milk boil over.
4. When the milk is almost gone and the rice is soft, turn off the heat and stir in the almond. Pour into a serving bowl and serve warm.

21

From

Poland

HOLIDAY COOKIES
Makes 2 dozen

Holidays are here. Time for getting together with friends to make traditional treats. In Poland these butter cookies are often star-shaped but you can make them any shape you like by using cookie cutters, jar lids, or by shaping the dough with a knife. After cutting the cookies, bake them, decorate them and wait—don't eat them all up! These cookies are for hanging, too. Where? On a tree, near a window, in a doorway—to say happy holidays!

INGREDIENTS

1 cup soft butter
1 cup confectioners' sugar
1 egg
1 t. vanilla
2½ cups flour
2 T. butter for greasing cookie sheets

For Glaze
2 T. hot water
1 cup sifted confectioners' sugar
½ t. your favorite flavoring
cookie decorations such as sprinkles, candy bits, etc.

EQUIPMENT

mixing bowl
mixing spoon
measuring cups
measuring spoons
rolling pin
wooden pastry board (optional)
cookie cutters or jar lids

knife for cutting cookie shapes
2 cookie sheets
string for hanging cookies or a straw to make holes for hanging cookies
wire racks

HOW TO MAKE:

1. Thoroughly cream the butter and sugar. Add the egg, vanilla and flour to make the dough. Mix well.
2. Use your hands to form a ball of dough. If the dough is too sticky, mix in a little more flour. Wrap the dough in waxed paper and chill in the freezer or refrigerator until firm.
3. Place the dough on a lightly floured board or table. (It's a good idea to work with ½ of the dough and leave the other ½ in the refrigerator until you're ready to use it.)
4. Roll the dough ¼ inch thick. If the dough sticks to the rolling pin, dust the rolling pin with flour.
5. Preheat oven to 325° F.
6. Grease the cookie sheets with the butter.
7. Cut out cookies and place them 1 inch apart on the cookie sheets.
8. To hang your cookies: Use a straw to punch a hole near the top of each cookie or make loops by cutting 3-inch lengths of string, folding them double and pressing the cut ends into the underside of each cookie near the top.
9. Bake the cookies 10 minutes or until lightly browned.
10. Cool on wire racks.
11. Glaze and decorate the cookies. To make the glaze: Mix together the boiling water and confectioners' sugar. Stir in the flavoring. Brush the glaze on the cookies. Sprinkle the decorations over the glaze.

From

Germany
PRETZEL A B C'S

Makes 20 pretzels

You can write your name with pretzels. Bend and twist the dough into shape, and you'll be carrying on the old German tradition of sculpting with dough. In Germany, every bakeshop boasts an artistic assortment of pretzels, horns, crescents, and other bread shapes. Try your hand at German bread "art."

INGREDIENTS

1½ cups lukewarm water
1   package yeast
4   cups flour
1   T. sugar
1   t. salt

2   T. butter to grease cookie sheets
1   egg
1   T. water
⅓ cup coarse salt

EQUIPMENT

large mixing bowl
measuring cups
measuring spoons
small mixing bowl
mixing spoon
wooden board to knead the dough (optional)

2 cookie sheets
pastry brush or paint brush
small bowl
wire racks

HOW TO MAKE:

1. In the large mixing bowl, place the lukewarm water and pour in the package of yeast. Let mixture sit about 5 minutes until bubbly.
2. In the small mixing bowl combine the flour, sugar, and salt. Add the sugar, salt and 3 cups of the flour to the yeast mixture. Stir until the ingredients are blended and form a ball.
3. Place the dough on a lightly floured board or tabletop.
4. Dust your hands with flour and begin kneading the dough. (See illustrations, page 43.) Slowly knead in the fourth cup of flour. After about 5 minutes the dough should be smooth and not sticky. This means you have kneaded enough.
5. Pull the dough into 20 pieces. Roll each into a long snake about ½ inch thick and 15 inches long.
6. Shape the dough into letters of the alphabet or into pretzel shapes.
7. Preheat the oven to 425° F.
8. Grease the cookie sheets with a small amount of butter and place the pretzels on the cookie sheets, allowing several inches of space between them.
9. In the small bowl combine the egg with 1 tablespoon of water and mix well. Paint the mixture on each pretzel and sprinkle with coarse salt.
10. Bake the pretzels for 20 minutes. Remove from oven and cool on wire racks.

From

the Soviet Union

NOODLE-AND-CHEESE CASSEROLE

Serves 6 to 8

Are you a noodle lover? If so, you're not alone. Italians love them and so do the Chinese; and Americans eat oodles of noodles of all kinds. In the Ukraine, which is part of the Soviet Union, rich egg noodles are the basis of many everyday dishes. The necessary flour and eggs are plentiful there as are fresh cottage cheese and sour cream. Make this common Ukrainian casserole with broad flat noodles. Serve it with thick slices of dark bread as the Ukrainians do.

INGREDIENTS

- 12 oz. box broad egg noodles (makes about 4 cups of cooked noodles)
- boiling water
- 3 eggs
- 4 T. sugar
- ½ cup sour cream
- ½ stick soft butter or margarine
- 1 cup cottage cheese
- ½ cup milk
- 1½ cups raisins (golden, brown, or a mixture of both kinds)
- 1 T. butter to grease baking dish or pan

EQUIPMENT

- large pot to cook the noodles
- medium mixing bowl
- fork or egg beater
- measuring cups
- measuring spoons
- mixing spoon
- casserole dish or baking pan

HOW TO MAKE:

1. Cook the noodles in boiling water according to package directions.
2. While the noodles are cooking, beat together the eggs and the sugar in the mixing bowl.
3. Add the sour cream, margarine, cottage cheese, milk, and raisins and mix well.
4. Drain the noodles and mix them with the cottage cheese mixture.
5. Preheat the oven to 350° F.
6. Grease the casserole dish or baking pan with butter and pour the mixture evenly into it.
7. Bake in the center of the oven for 30 to 40 minutes until the noodles start to brown.

From
Indonesia
COCONUT CHICKEN
Serves 6 🍴🍴

Have a *rijsttafel*—that means rice table—a unique Indonesian way of eating. Here's how Indonesians do it. First they make a pot of fluffy rice. (See page vii for directions.) Then they prepare an assortment of meats, vegetables, and relishes. Indonesian cooks are careful to vary the tastes between spicy and bland, hot and cold, crisp and soft, sweet and sour. For the one rule in planning a *rijsttafel* is: Flavors should not be repeated.

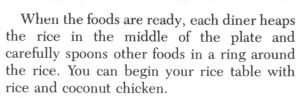

When the foods are ready, each diner heaps the rice in the middle of the plate and carefully spoons other foods in a ring around the rice. You can begin your rice table with rice and coconut chicken.

INGREDIENTS

1	chicken (3 lb.) cut in serving pieces	⅛	t. cayenne
3	cups coconut milk (Coconut milk is available at health-food stores.)	¼	t. salt
		5	mint leaves
		1	medium onion

EQUIPMENT

paper towels
deep frying pan, large enough to hold the chicken
measuring spoons

measuring cups
paring knife
baking or broiling pan
cooking fork or kitchen tongs

HOW TO MAKE:

1. Wash the chicken and dry it with paper towels.
2. Place the chicken in the frying pan. Add the coconut milk, cayenne, salt, and mint leaves.
3. Cut up the onion into small pieces and add to the frying pan.
4. Bring the chicken and other ingredients to a boil. Then turn down the heat and simmer for 20 minutes or until the liquid is nearly gone and only thick sauce remains.
5. Preheat the broiler.
6. Remove the chicken from the frying pan and put it into the baking or broiling pan. Save the sauce.
7. Broil the chicken for 20 to 30 minutes. Use the cooking fork or tongs to turn the chicken while it cooks so that it does not burn.
8. When chicken is done, transfer it to a platter and pour the sauce over it. Serve.

China
WON TON SOUP
Makes 100 won tons

Soup last—that's how the Chinese often serve it. First they serve the appetizers, then the many main dishes, and last, a hearty soup. Won ton soup can also be served by itself as a main dish. Give each diner about 10 won tons and pour the hot broth over them. Of course, won tons need not be eaten in soup at all. Deep-fry or pan-fry them for an appetizer. No matter how you choose to cook them, you'll like won tons from beginning to end.

INGREDIENTS

1   lb. package won-ton wrappers (about 100 wrappers)
1   lb. ground pork (about 2 cups)
½   package frozen chopped spinach, thawed and water drained off.
1   t. ginger root
1   egg
1   t. salt
1   T. Chinese soy sauce
1   T. sesame-seed oil (You can also use peanut or corn oil.)

Soup for 4 People
4-6 cups chicken broth   1 scallion

EQUIPMENT

measuring cups
paring knife
measuring spoons
mixing bowl
mixing spoon
glass
large plate or tray

damp kitchen towel or paper towels
large pot for cooking won tons
medium pot for heating chicken broth
slotted spoon

HOW TO MAKE:

1. To make the filling: Cut off a large slice of ginger root, peel it, and mince it.
2. Combine the pork, ginger root, egg, salt, soy sauce, and oil.
3. Stir in the chopped spinach.
4. To assemble the won tons: First fill the glass with cold water. Have the large plate or tray and damp towel ready.
5. Place 1 heaping teaspoon of filling below the center of each won-ton wrapper (see drawings). Roll the lower corner over the filling. Take the two ends and pull them down until they meet and overlap. Dip a finger in the glass of water and moisten one end of the wrapper. Pinch the ends together to seal. The won ton will look like a nurse's cap.
6. Place the finished won tons on the plate or tray and cover with the damp towel or paper towel until ready to cook. Keep the filled won-ton wrappers also covered so that they do not dry out.
7. Keep filling and rolling won tons until you have made the desired amount. You can freeze uncooked won tons as well as any leftover filling and wrappers.
8. To cook the won tons: Bring about 2 quarts of water to a boil in the large pot. Drop in 20 or so of the won tons. Bring to a boil again. Simmer for 5 minutes. Remove won tons with the slotted spoon. Continue until all are cooked.
9. To serve won ton soup. Mince the scallion. Bring the chicken broth to a boil. Place small amount of scallion and cooked won tons in individual soup bowls. Pour in the hot chicken broth and serve.

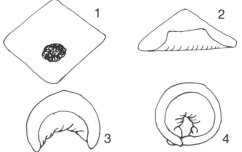

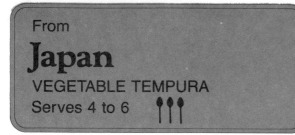

From

Japan

VEGETABLE TEMPURA
Serves 4 to 6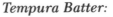

Japanese chefs have many secrets. Food should be simple and light, they say. In Japan, the cook is an artist who arranges food beautifully to please the eye. Vegetable tempura is a delicate treat which tastes just as good as it looks.

Tempura can be an appetizer or main course. To make it you need a high-sided frying pan or deep-fat fryer. (See page vii for directions.) Ask an adult for help with the frying.

SECRETS FOR PERFECT TEMPURA:
Have all vegetables cut and ready before you start to cook.
The batter must be ice-cold.
Remove loose bits of food and batter from the hot oil during the cooking process.

INGREDIENTS

½ lb. of fresh vegetables for each person for a main course. Select any of the following and cut into bite-sized pieces: carrots, celery, eggplant, beans, mushrooms, squash, green pepper, cucumber, broccoli, cauliflower, parsley.

Dipping Sauce:
1 cup soy sauce or 1 cup Japanese *dashi* (fish stock) boiled with ¼ cup soy sauce. Let cool before serving.

Tempura Batter:
The batter should be so thin that the color of the cooked food shows through.

2 eggs	¾ cup flour
1 cup ice water	

The oil
Vegetable oil for frying should be at least 1½ inches deep.

EQUIPMENT

paring knife	kitchen tongs
mixing bowl	slotted spoon or
measuring cups	strainer (optional)
mixing spoon	paper towels
frying pan or	oven mitts
deep-fat fryer	

HOW TO MAKE:

1. Wash and slice all the vegetables.
2. Prepare the batter by combining the eggs, ice water, and flour. Stir only until blended. If you stir too much, the batter will become sticky. Dip vegetables into batter.
3. In the frying pan or deep-fat fryer, heat the oil to 380° F. The oil is ready when a drop of batter sinks to the center and quickly floats back to the surface.
4. Using the kitchen tongs, drop several vegetable pieces into the oil. Don't overload the pan. Fry for 1 or 2 minutes. Remove the cooked food with the tongs or slotted spoon or small strainer. Drain on paper towels.
5. Continue frying vegetables, several pieces at a time. Remember to remove any stray bits of batter.
6. Serve immediately. Each person should have a small bowl of dipping sauce. Pick the tempura up with chopsticks and dip it into the sauce.

From
Korea
SESAME BEEF
Serves 4 ♠♠♠

Koreans make this tasty barbecued beef outdoors over a small charcoal burner. However, it is just as delicious cooked indoors in a broiler or frying pan. Either way, the sesame flavor, found in many Korean recipes, comes through—nutty and delicious.

To Make Crushed, Toasted Sesame Seeds:

Place sesame seeds in a frying pan over medium heat. Cook, stirring constantly until golden brown. To crush seeds: (1) put them into a blender, or (2) crush them in a mortar with a pestle, or (3) crush them in a wooden bowl with the back of a spoon.

INGREDIENTS

1   pound flank steak
2   scallions (optional)
1   clove garlic
2   T. crushed, toasted sesame seeds

2   T. sesame oil or vegetable oil
¼   cup soy sauce

EQUIPMENT

sharp knife
small bowl
measuring spoons
measuring cups

shallow pan to hold the steak
4-6 metal skewers (if grilling or broiling)

HOW TO MAKE:

1. Slice the steak very thin across the grain (see drawing). Cut steak strips into 3-inch-long pieces.
2. Slice the scallions thinly into small rounds.
3. Peel the garlic clove and mince.
4. In the small bowl combine the scallions, garlic, sesame seeds, oil, and soy sauce.
5. Place the pieces of steak in a shallow pan and pour the seasonings over the meat. Turn the steak to coat with the marinade. Marinate at least 1 hour.
6. To cook, thread the pieces of steak on skewers. Grill or broil for about 2 minutes on each side. The meat should be crisply browned but not burned. (If you are cooking the meat in a frying pan, cook over medium-high heat for 5 minutes on each side.)

From
Vietnam
CHICKEN-LONG RICE SOUP
Serves 4 to 6

Rice is the main food in the Vietnamese diet. Served boiled, fried, or made into noodles, rice appears at every meal. This dish consists of shredded chicken, bits of scallion, and a special cellophane noodle called "long rice," all served in a flavorful broth. You can buy "long rice" noodles in Oriental food stores. Otherwise, you can use Italian vermicelli.

INGREDIENTS

- ½ lb. "long rice" (cellophane noodles or vermicelli)
- 2 scallions
- 5 cups chicken broth
- 1 T. soy sauce
- salt and pepper to taste
- 1 large chicken breast

EQUIPMENT

large serving bowl
knife
medium saucepan
measuring cups
measuring spoons
mixing spoon

HOW TO MAKE:

1. Place the chicken breast in the saucepan and add enough water to cover it. Bring the water to a boil and cook for three minutes. Lower the heat, cover, and simmer for 20 to 30 minutes. Remove chicken breast, and let cool. Then skin and slice into thin strips.
2. If using "long rice," soak in warm water for 10 minutes. Drain. Break into pieces. If using other noodles, cook until tender following package directions.
3. Pile noodles in a large serving bowl.
4. Finely chop the scallions, both green and white parts.
5. Bring the chicken broth to a boil in the saucepan. Stir in the soy sauce. Season with salt and pepper. Add the cooked chicken strips and chopped scallions and cook for 1 minute over medium heat.
6. Pour the soup over the noodles. Serve hot.

30

Time for a snack. Have a fried banana, Philippine style. These banana chips are often dipped in batter and then fried. Or you can simply slice and fry them quickly in oil.(See page vii for directions.) Bananas thrive in tropical climates, so it's no wonder they crop up in Philippine foods as often as they do—in soups, stews, desserts, and snacks.

INGREDIENTS

6	bananas	salt
	oil for deep frying	

EQUIPMENT

knife	slotted spoon
deep-fat fryer or	oven mitts
high-sided frying pan	paper towels

HOW TO MAKE:

If you have not had experience with deep-fat frying, be sure to ask an adult or older friend to help.

1. Peel the bananas and cut into ½-inch slices.
2. Heat the oil until it bubbles. (NOTE: For deep-fat frying, turn to page vii.)
3. Carefully drop several slices at a time into the hot oil and fry until golden brown. Use oven mitts to protect your hands.
4. Remove cooked bananas with a slotted spoon and drain on paper towels.
5. Sprinkle with salt and serve hot.

NOTE: This works best with plantains, which are green and less sweet than yellow bananas. Look for plantains in South American or Spanish markets.

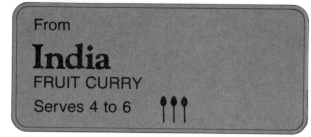

From

India
FRUIT CURRY

Serves 4 to 6

What's for dinner in India? The answer to this question is often curry, a spicy dish served with rice. There are many different kinds of curries—most have fish, meat, or vegetables, or a combination of these. Ours is a unique version made of vegetables and fruit, which is especially delicious. The one thing all curries have in common is curry powder, a zesty seasoning made up of many herbs and spices: ground mustard, coriander, chili powder, black pepper, ground cumin, fenugreek, ginger, and garlic.

INGREDIENTS

2	onions	¼	cup raisins
2	tomatoes	½	t. salt
1	orange	¼	t. curry powder,
1	banana		or to taste
1	green pepper	2	cups cooked rice
3	T. butter		(For directions
2	T. sunflower seeds		see page vii)

EQUIPMENT

paring knife   measuring spoons
large frying pan   mixing spoon

HOW TO MAKE:

1. Peel and cut into pieces the onions, tomatoes, orange, and banana. Chop the green pepper.
2. Melt the butter in the frying pan. Add the onions and green pepper and stir until soft. Add the tomatoes, orange, banana, sunflower seeds, raisins, salt, curry powder. Cook, stirring, for 5 minutes.
3. Stir the cooked rice into the mixture and simmer for 5 minutes, stirring constantly. Serve.

Pakistan

DERAM FITI—
Wheat-sprout Pancakes

Makes 10 to 12 pancakes

Happy One Hundredth Birthday! A rare occasion? Not to the Hunzas. Many of these mountain people live to celebrate their hundredth birthdays. Some live to be even older. People say that the Hunza diet has a lot to do with their long lives. At a Hunza birthday party the food might be *Deram Fiti*. It is made with dried wheat sprouts, ground into flour and cooked like pancakes. Try our version of this dish made with fresh wheat sprouts.

INGREDIENTS

¾ cup whole wheat flour	1¼ cups milk
½ cup white flour	2 T. butter
1 t. baking powder	2 T. honey
¼ t. baking soda	1 T. wheat sprouts (see note)
¼ t. salt	3 T. butter for cooking pancakes
2 eggs	

EQUIPMENT

2 mixing bowls	fork or egg beater
mixing spoon	small saucepan
measuring cups	frying pan
measuring spoons	spatula

HOW TO MAKE:

1. Combine the whole wheat flour, white flour, baking powder, baking soda, and salt in a mixing bowl.
2. In a small saucepan, melt 2 T. butter.
3. In the other mixing bowl, lightly beat the eggs.
4. Add the milk, melted butter, and honey to the beaten eggs and mix well.
5. Pour the milk and egg mixture into the dry ingredients.
6. Stir in the wheat sprouts.
7. To cook, melt 1 tablespoon of butter in the frying pan over medium heat.
8. Use the mixing spoon to put a small amount of batter for each pancake into the frying pan. The pancakes will be 3 to 4 inches in diameter.
9. Cook the pancakes until bubbles appear on top.
10. Turn each pancake over with the spatula and cook until evenly browned.
11. Serve the pancakes hot, topped with the syrup, honey, powdered sugar, or fruit.

NOTE: You can buy wheat sprouts in a health-food store. Or, you can grow seeds yourself: Soak 1 tablespoon of wheat-sprout seeds in a dish of water. Put a colander in the sink. Pour the sprouts and water into the colander. Let the water drip out. Cover the colander with a clean dish towel. Every day run water over the sprouts in the colander and then cover with a dish towel. In about three days the sprouts will begin to grow, and in five days they will be ready to eat.

Iraq

YOGURT SOUP

Serves 6

In A.D. 679 some of the leading Middle Eastern doctors brought out a manuscript. In it they said, "Yogurt is good for strengthening the stomach and refreshing the intestinal tract." Even earlier, this ancient food was thought to have health-giving qualities. Iraqis still think so. Yogurt is an important part of the Iraqi diet. So sip some health the way they do in Iraq.

INGREDIENTS

¼ cup seedless raisins	3 cups plain yogurt
1 cup boiling water	½ cup milk
1 cup cold water	2 t. salt
1 cucumber	½ t. pepper
	1 t. dill weed

EQUIPMENT

measuring cups
small bowl
paring knife

medium-sized mixing bowl
measuring spoons
mixing spoon

HOW TO MAKE:

1. Boil water. Put raisins into bowl and pour boiling water over them to soften. Drain carefully.
2. Add cold water to the bowl and chill in the refrigerator for 1 hour.
3. Peel cucumber. Chop it into small pieces and put into a mixing bowl. Add yogurt, milk, salt, pepper and dill weed. Stir.
4. Add raisins and water to the mixture and stir.
5. Chill for an hour in the refrigerator and serve.

Light a candle. See, it glows. Spin a dreidl. Round it goes. It's the first night of Hanukkah and as part of this holiday night many families make *latkes*, the traditional dish for Hanukkah. Serve these crisp potato pancakes with applesauce, jam, or sour cream.

INGREDIENTS

5	potatoes
1	onion
2	eggs
3	T. flour or matzo meal

salt and pepper to taste
½ cup vegetable oil
applesauce, jam, or sour cream

EQUIPMENT

paring knife
peeler
small bowl
fork
grater

mixing spoon
measuring spoons
frying pan
spatula
paper towels

HOW TO MAKE:

1. Wash the potatoes and peel them. Grate them fine.
2. Peel and chop the onion.
3. Lightly beat the eggs in a small bowl.
4. Place the potatoes, onion, and eggs in a mixing bowl and blend well.
5. Add flour, salt and pepper. Stir.
6. To cook, pour a small amount of oil into the frying pan and heat over medium heat.
7. Drop large spoonfuls of batter into the frying pan. Cook until brown on one side, about 2 minutes. Turn and brown on the other side. Drain on paper towels.
8. Add more oil to the frying pan and cook another batch of pancakes. Continue until all the batter has been used.
9. Serve the pancakes with applesauce, jam, or sour cream.

From
Tunisia

HONEY-DIPPED DOUGHNUTS

Makes about
10 small doughnuts

Imagine you are in a market street in Tunisia. It teems with people who are talking, selling, buying, and eating. You come to the corner. What do you see? Likely a dozen or more vendors with their wares on display. One woman has a basket bursting with a pyramid of rainbow-colored fruit. A man holds a tray covered with a gay print cloth. On top are little pastries piled high. A boy sits cross-legged next to a cart filled with honey-dipped doughnuts. Try one.

INGREDIENTS

2	eggs
¼	cup vegetable oil
½	cup sugar
¼	cup orange juice
1	orange
2	cups flour

1	T. baking soda
3	cups vegetable oil for frying
¼	cup flour for shaping doughnuts
1	cup honey

EQUIPMENT

mixing bowl
measuring cups
mixing spoon
grater
flour sifter
measuring spoons

high-sided
  saucepan or
  deep-fat fryer
kitchen tongs
paper towels
small saucepan

HOW TO MAKE:

If you have not had experience with deep-fat frying, be sure to ask an adult or older friend to help.

1. Mix the eggs, oil, sugar, and orange juice in the mixing bowl.
2. Grate the orange rind. Add the grated rind to the mixture.
3. Sift the flour and baking soda, and add to the egg-and-orange mixture.
4. Beat until thick and smooth. The batter will be elastic.
5. Cover and set aside for about ½ hour.
6. Dip your hands in the flour and lift dough from the bowl. Pull the dough apart into 10 pieces.
7. Roll each piece of dough into a ball. Flatten the ball and poke a hole through it with a finger. You'll need to keep your hands well floured.
8. Heat the oil in the saucepan or deep-fat fryer. The oil should not fill so much of the pan so that it will boil over when the doughnuts are added. (NOTE: For deep-fat frying, see page vii.)
9. Put two doughnuts at a time into the oil and fry for 30 seconds. Use the tongs to turn the doughnuts and fry 30 seconds more. The doughnuts should be golden brown.
10. Remove the doughnuts with the tongs and drain on the paper towels.
11. When all the doughnuts are cooked, warm the honey in a saucepan.
12. Using the tongs, dip each doughnut into the honey.
13. Place the doughnuts on a plate. These are best eaten while still warm.

From
Senegal
COUSCOUS
Serves 6

Share this tasty dish from Senegal with friends of yours. It's made with couscous, a type of fine semolina made from wheat grain. Couscous is eaten in many Senegalese homes almost every evening. Each family has its own special way of making it. But all agree: each grain should swell and become light, soft, velvety, and separate from its neighbor.

After making our version of couscous, you might vary the ingredients to your own taste. Try adding zucchini, lamb, raisins, green pepper, or fish.

INGREDIENTS

1	cup water	4	T. butter
1	cup couscous (Couscous can be found in most supermarkets.)	1	small can chick peas
		1	bay leaf
		⅛	t. garlic powder
1	onion	½	cup chicken broth
1	green pepper	½	t. dill weed
1	tomato	1	T. soy sauce
1	carrot		

EQUIPMENT

measuring cups   paring knife
saucepan   large frying pan
mixing spoon   spatula

HOW TO MAKE:

1. Pour the water into the saucepan. Bring to a boil. Add the couscous. Turn heat to simmer and stir for 3 to 4 minutes until water is gone and couscous is light and fluffy. Set aside.
2. Prepare the fresh vegetables. Cut up the onion, green pepper, tomato, and carrot into small pieces. Slice the mushrooms the long way into several pieces.
3. Melt the butter in the frying pan. Add the fresh vegetables except for the mushrooms and sauté over medium heat for 5 minutes.
4. Add the mushrooms, chick peas, bay leaf, garlic powder, chicken broth, dill weed, and soy sauce to the frying pan.
5. Continue cooking 5 minutes more. The vegetables are done when they are cooked through but not mushy.
6. Place the couscous in a serving dish. Spoon the vegetables over the couscous and serve.

From
Mali
VEGIE RICE
Serves 4 to 6

INGREDIENTS

1	cup long-grained rice	3	T. butter
1	tomato	1	T. tomato paste
1	cup mushrooms	⅛	t. salt
1	green pepper		dash of cayenne
1	small onion	¼	t. curry powder

EQUIPMENT

measuring cups
paring knife
measuring spoons

large skillet
cooking fork or mixing
   spoon

HOW TO MAKE:

1. Cook the rice. (For directions see page vii.)
2. Wash the tomato, mushrooms, and green pepper. Cut the tomato into thin wedges, cut the mushrooms in half, and mince the green pepper.
3. Peel and slice the onion.
4. Melt the butter in the skillet. Sauté the onion until soft. Add the other vegetables, tomato paste, salt, cayenne, and curry powder.
5. Cook for 15 minutes, stirring.
6. Stir in the cooked rice and serve.

An old African saying goes, "The sun is but an egg that hatches great things." So believes the West African farmer who lives on those vegetables and grains enriched by the sun. You can vary the vegetables in this recipe. If you use any of the following, you will still have an authentic Mali mixture: yams, peas, beans, or eggplant.

Make a mix of fresh fruit. You'll have a typical African dessert. Sprinkle the fruit with chopped peanuts. To eat, spear fruit on skewers or forks and dip into this tangy sauce.

INGREDIENTS

Choose as many fruits in season as you wish for a colorful mix.

watermelon
cantaloupe
papaya
mangoes
tangerines
oranges
apples
strawberries
pineapple
bananas
½ cup peanuts

For Dip

1 can frozen lemonade, thawed

1 cup coconut cream (available in gourmet markets and health-food stores)

EQUIPMENT

sharp knife
chopper
plate for serving

small bowl for
serving dip

HOW TO MAKE:

1. Cut the fruit into small pieces (except for the pineapple and bananas).
2. Peel the bananas and slice in half-inch pieces.
3. Cut the pineapple into wedges (see drawing p. 43).
4. Chop the peanuts.
5. Arrange the fruit on a plate and sprinkle with peanuts.
6. To make the dip, mix the lemonade and coconut cream.
7. Serve the dip with the fruit platter.

From

Tanzania
GROUNDNUT CRUNCH
Makes 15 1-inch balls

East Africans rarely munch on sweets, but when they do, groundnuts, or peanuts as we call them, are always included. Groundnuts are the main ingredient of many African foods. If you and your friends like to munch, try sharing Groundnut Crunch.

INGREDIENTS

¼ lb. unsalted peanuts
⅓ cup water

⅓ cup sugar
½ t. cinnamon

EQUIPMENT

chopper or sharp knife
chopping board
measuring cups
measuring spoons

heavy-bottomed saucepan
wooden spoon
waxed paper

HOW TO MAKE:

1. Shell the peanuts and chop them fine.
2. In a heavy-bottomed saucepan heat the water and sugar over low heat, stirring constantly until the sugar dissolves.
3. Add the peanuts and cinnamon and continue stirring for about 3 minutes until the sugar turns light brown. Be careful that the mixture doesn't burn.
4. Remove the pan from the heat and let cool about 10 minutes until cool enough to handle but still soft.
5. Pick up bits of the mixture and shape into 1-inch balls. Place on waxed paper until set.

41

Kenya

BANANA SMOOTHIE

Makes 2 drinks

Blend two bananas, and make some great shakes. Here's a refreshing drink to share with a friend on any picnic or safari.

INGREDIENTS

2	bananas	1	cup orange juice
1	cup plain yogurt	4	T. honey

EQUIPMENT

knife	measuring cups
blender or jar with	measuring spoons
lid	2 tall glasses

HOW TO MAKE:

1. Slice the bananas. If you don't have a blender, mash the bananas with a fork.
2. In the blender or jar, blend the bananas with the rest of the ingredients.
3. Pour into two tall glasses. Add ice if you like a cold smoothie.

Special Instructions

HOW TO KNEAD DOUGH

1. Push the heels of your hands into the dough and away from your body. (Use one hand if this is more comfortable.)
2. Fold the dough over toward you.
3. Turn the dough ¼ of the way around.
4. Push again with the heels of your hands. Continue pushing, folding, and turning until the dough is smooth and satiny.

HOW TO CUT A PINEAPPLE

1. Lay fruit on its side and slice off leafy top and base with a sharp knife (ask an adult to help).
2. Divide the fruit into quarters.
3. Cut the triangular core away from each quarter.
4. Lay each quarter on its side and slice into wedges.

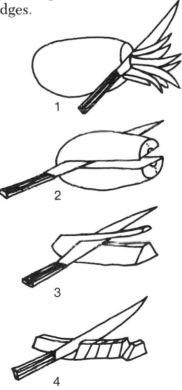

Metric and U. S. Measure Index

The system of measurement used in the United States is different from the metric system most countries use. In the U.S. the liquid measure of one cup is used to measure both liquid and dry ingredients. The metric system measures dry ingredients by weight (grams and kilograms) and liquids by milliliters and liters. This difference makes it hard to convert from U.S. to metric measures with complete accuracy. However, listed here are some U.S. measures and their approximate metric equivalents.

Liquid Measure

U.S.	Metric
1 ounce	about 30 milliliters
½ cup	about 120 milliliters
1 cup	about ¼ liter
1 quart	about 1 liter

(Remember, there are 8 ounces in one U.S. cup and 32 ounces in one quart. If you want to be more precise, 1 ounce is 29.57 milliliters.)

Dry Measure

U.S.	Metric
1 ounce	about 28 grams
8 ounces	about 225 grams
1 pound	about 450 grams

(Remember, there are 16 ounces in a U.S. pound. If you want to be more precise, 1 ounce is 28.35 grams.)

Index